THE CAREFUL VOTER'S DICTIONARY OF LANGUAGE POLLUTION

(*Understanding Willietalk and Other Spinspeak*)

by James Baar

1st edition (expanded)

Copyright © 1999 by James Baar

ISBN 1-58500-078-7

Protect yourself from spin docs, pols, fanatics, business titans, lawyers, academics and other worthies who are willfully befogging language to muddle your brain. Orwell knew what snake oil can do. So did Plato. So did Stalin. So did Hitler. Spin rots the mind.

Here are hundreds of helpful definitions of polluted words and phrases in current use including: alone, courtesy call, customer satisfaction, defining moment, rightsizing, investment, the rich, the poor, the children, mean spirited, sexual relations, alternative turkey, liberty impaired and values clarification. The Dictionary arms you with an intellectual scalpel for de-layering the thick cosmetic overlay of public communications that obscures the real world.

Also included is a short history of language pollution, a selection of great examples of polluted words of the recent past, and a Glossary of Technical Terms such as plastertalk, willietalk, bravebabble, Halloweentalk, tin-eartalk and Trojan-horse construction.

This book is designed to help any careful voter who yearns for a world where, regardless of what anyone swears under oath, that, in the words of T.S. Eliot, "a cat is not a dog."

Other books by James Baar

Fiction
The Great Free Enterprise Gambit

Nonfiction (Co-author)
Polaris!

Combat Missileman

The English language today is being polluted almost beyond recognition from what it was in the middle of the 20th Century. In fact, as the Century ends, American English is undergoing an Orwellian catastrophe.

When Alice met Humpty Dumpty on her famous excursion through the looking-glass, he told her that when he used a word it meant "just what I choose it to mean." If Alice were to visit Washington today and she happened to see an elephant on the Mall or in the Lincoln Bedroom, Humpty Dumpty in all probability would tell her that what she saw was a St. Bernard; she should feel perfectly safe to take it home with her; it could sleep by the fireside when it wasn't saving travelers lost in the snow.

This may sound mildly humorous at best; silly at worst. It also is very serious; in fact, it is potentially deadly to human reasoning.

Think what happens, to stay with Alice's problem, when you no longer deal with the elephant based on several thousands years of accumulated experience in dealing with elephants; when, instead, you draw on the world's accumulated experience in dealing with St. Bernards. First, you put a barrel of whiskey under the elephant's chin; then you take it home to sit by the fire; then you take it up in the mountains to help travelers lost in the passes. You are dismayed, of course, to find that your St. Bernard a.k.a. Jumbo, (now called José to reflect diversity) is failing to perform well. But you keep trying. Studies are conducted. There is much argument about what to do to solve the problem. Possibly, better training is needed. Possibly, better adjustment can be sought through psychiatric aid. Possibly, your St. Bernard, in consideration of the unfortunate socio-economic environment in which he was raised, just needs to be given more chances. Obviously, more funding is

3

needed. And obviously we will need to educate people to be more tolerant when your St. Bernard tramples their automobiles during its morning walks.

Soon another interesting phenomenon occurs. People are beginning to wonder and argue about the St. Bernards that do curl up by fires and do provide whiskey to lost travelers. These St. Bernards begin to look funny. Why are they so stunted? Where are their long trunks? Where are their tusks? The obvious result: more studies, more argument, more need for tolerance. (It is not fair to point out that the St. Bernard is different from other St. Bernards just because it was born without a trunk. Those who do that are being racist and hateful. This St. Bernard clearly is a victim.)

The real problem here, of course, is language pollution: the continuing corruption of words in order to describe and build a world closer to our heart's desire. If you have just arrived from Mars, you don't care what Humpty Dumpty says. To paraphrase T.S. Eliot's poem about differentiating cats and dogs, an elephant is not a St. Bernard.

Words are the coin of thought. When we debase this currency and move from gold-standard words to lead-standard words to papier-mâché words, we debase our ability for rational discussion; our ability to think, to make logical judgments, to solve problems. Instead, we increasingly spend our time studying and arguing about fantasy models of the real world. We are back in Plato's famous cave. The actors cast highly distorted shadows on the wall. That is what we see; never the real players. We think the often very distorted shadows are reality and try to deal with them.

Today we build these fantasy models through rampant use of euphemisms, adjusted definitions and re-minted portmanteau words. If the name for our idea has negative baggage, we name it something more positive or more vague or both. If we find the name for the opposition's idea has too many positive connotations, we name it something much more negative. Or we simply make and insist on 180 degree Orwellian claims such as war is peace. Soon we are mentally blinded and lost in a blizzard of fuzzball words. We argue with them. We hurl them at each other. We build our plans and proposals out of them. Refusal to use them is ridiculed, hated, shouted down. Our knowledge systems are increasingly impaired. Resulting policy based on and using this fuzzball language may improve the fantasy models but seldom the real world except by happenstance. In fact, the effect is often quite the opposite.

The first step in combating the language pollution that is befogging and besmirching our intellectual climate and crippling policy formation is to recognize it and understand the process that creates it.

There has always been some degree of natural pollution along with decay or gradual change of meaning. This is how language has evolved. But the pollution we experience today goes far beyond mere natural, evolutionary development of new shades of meaning, the introduction of new words and the loss or evolutionary corruption of old ones. It involves the deliberate, aggressive continuing practice -- and its conscious and unconscious acceptance -- of the introduction and use of misleading words and phrases that distort meaning and reality. The ultimate result of this is the destruction of communication.

The practice of deliberate language pollution takes a variety of forms. Here are some of them:

• Use of 60's-type "gooey talk" words such as caring; its antonym, mean-spirited; sexual preference (sodomy); single mother (career welfare-supported bearer of numerous illegitimate children); economically vulnerable (poor);

societally impaired (pathological killer); pro-choice (abortion on demand).

- Use of technical neologisms such as ethnic diversity (generally non-Western Civilization); value neutral (totally amoral); Native American (Stone Age Asian aborigines who took over North and South America several thousand years ago as opposed to Europeans who started taking over 500 years ago.)

- Use of euphemisms once, twice or even three-times removed such as people of color (anyone whose skin is a few shades darker than white except for Jews and pureblooded Iberians.): physically challenged (no legs); mentally challenged (22 IQ); exceptional children (14 IQ). These include portmanteau gift wrap names that glorify a package of rather mundane or less exciting items. e.g., middle class bill of rights for some mostly me-too tax cuts..

- Use of antithesis words such as contribution for tax; spending cut for fees; choice for abortion, investment for spending.

- Use of motherhood words such as hardworking middle class, sacrifice, love of country, freedom, democracy, family and right to (whatever) as the facade of word castles that often house totally contrary and inimical proposals.

- Use of new positive *spin* meanings for old positive words such as working class (middle class), communications (public relations) and sexual orientation (you name it).

All of these categories along with others have words that carry manipulative, misleading *spin* no matter how horrendous the underlying truth. And to disagree, you are very bad. This process involves a total denial of reality: The enemy at the gate is an admiring group of well-wishers. Bubonic plague is really a bad cold. The rising river is nothing to be concerned about. The fellows with the guns and knives in the park are bucolic picnickers. The killers are victims. The robbers need healing.

Language pollution to some degree has been a disability of the human race for thousands of years. Under the Tang Dynasty in the seventh century the imperial bureaucracy created Standard Histories of the regime for the national archives. These histories, carefully fine tuned to imperial considerations, were called "Veritable Records." The fine tuning process was known officially as "appropriate concealment" and "ethical instruction."

The Communist Party and the Communist Soviet Union did much to pollute language throughout most of the 20th Century. Soviet leaders became adept at calling most of their failures the result of capitalist subversion. They invented the foiling of enemy conspiracies for the paranoid mass murder of the toiling masses for whom the Soviet Union was allegedly created; Marxist/Leninist reform for the enslavement of their peasants; the triumph of collective farming for the destruction of their agriculture; the workers paradise for the gulags, the inevitability of history for the insistence on demonstrably economic ineptitude. Under Stalin and his successors, the Soviets and their Communist followers around the world did particularly outstanding work in polluting language by minting antithesis words and gaining belief and acceptance of them through robotic repetition. Days before the total bankruptcy and collapse of the Communist Soviet Union, Pravda (Truth), continued to refer to disasters as difficulties.

Germany under Nazi leadership also did much to advance language pollution techniques – particularly the use of antithesis words -- during the happily foreshortened thousand years of the Third Reich. As Hitler said before the world paid much attention to him: "In the size of the lie

7

there is always contained a certain factor of credibility, since the great masses of the people...will more easily fall victim to a great lie than to a small one."

In the United States, many sources -- Corporate America, the Academy, the Military, Hollywood, and armies of Communist Russia admirers, arbitrary do-gooders, lawyers, indicted and unindicted charlatans and self-proclaimed leaders, public relations consultants, assorted mountebanks and snake oil peddlers -- have been busy polluting American English in the last half century. But, despite our national insistence on equality in all matters including talent, some in this area have greater capabilities than others. As the 20th Century ends, outstanding polluters of language appear 24 hours a day on national TV to explain that elephants are St. Bernards. Politicians, long adept in the arts of bamboozlement, can hardly wait to sign on to the latest fuzzball euphemism. The burgeoning Poverty Industry and the enriched graduates of the Sixties Age of Compassion deserve special mention for creativity. But surely President William Jefferson Clinton has proven himself a language polluter with few peers.

History certainly will show that much of the pollution of the language that preceded the Clinton Administration was prologue to the outstanding championship in the field provided to friends and foes by President Clinton. Clinton and the people around him did not invent language pollution, but they most certainly did much to perfect it and expand its usage. The practice of *willietalk* early on became the tool of choice for a President who made clear that he had no central core of beliefs other than the desire to be and stay in power, be liked and to enjoy the benefits of power. He demonstrated the soul of an advertising copywriter of the worst sort: whatever Clinton said was Instant Divine Truth, but not necessarily five minutes after he said it.

Months before coming to power, the Clinton Administration exhibited frightening adeptness at the outrageous, often pathological and continual use of euphemisms, quarter-truth slickisms and fuzz-land word castles to disguise and deny the truth and promote its nostrums and euphoric positions.

Often, as a result, public debate became irrelevant because it centered on the latest word castles being created rather than the facts of the real world. When the discussion is about a map of a world that doesn't exist, the decision about which road to take can only lead to futility and disaster. This is one of the great destructive characteristics of language pollution.

A collateral mind-fogging aspect of language pollution is the rationalization put forth by its devotees that when they fail to accomplish their objectives it is because they have done a poor job in delivering their messages. Their proposals have not been rejected because of their inherent value but only because the communications has not been quite up to snuff. Probably the most outrageous use of this technique was Clinton's rationalization of the Democratic loss of the 1994 congressional elections. At first he said that the American people voted for change and Clinton in 1992; then they voted for change again in 1994 because: 1. Clinton didn't bring on change fast enough. 2. He was guilty of poor message delivery on the great things that he had accomplished. Later, Clinton dropped #1 and fell back on #2 alone: If only a better job had been done communicating, all would have been well.

A second collateral aspect of language pollution, a tactic that is highly virulent as it can be highly successful, is to attack immediately and abrasively with polluted language anyone suggesting that language pollution is taking place. To suggest that "war" is not "peace" after all,

9

is to be hateful, divisive, extremist, go to far – probably all four.

Both of these aspects of language pollution were abundantly demonstrated in Clinton's successful reelection campaign. And reached flood stage in fighting the numerous criminal investigations of the Clinton presidency and striving to ward off impeachment and removal from office.

Fortunately for the future of the Republic, some modest recognition that corrective action is needed has set in. An increasing number of linguistically adept citizens, struggling in the miasma of *willietalk,* instinctively know a great truth: when we no longer can rely on the meaning of words, then the core structure of Western Thought that has made political freedom possible is threatened

To return to a linguistic gold standard, it is essential to recognize the Potemkin Village language being foisted on America and discount it. The following **Glossary** of technical terms and ***Dictionary*** of polluted words and phrases are designed to help you do just that.

Glossary of Technical Terms

willietalk = outrageous, often pathological and continual use of euphemisms, slickisms (quarter-truths) and blatant fuzzball words to promote oneself and various political nostrums and to disguise and/or deny the truth.

willielook = exaggerated and clearly fraudulent facial mannerisms such as misty eyes-on-command (funerals and thoughts of the disadvantaged), biting of lips (thoughts of the children, the aged, the sick) and Mussolini juttings of jaw (playing of national anthems and thoughts of military glory featuring no casualties) to emphasize particularly incredible slickisms.

goretalk = outrageously pretentious words and phrases chosen to obscure meaning and banality of thought and to attempt to provide an intellectual veneer. *goretalk* in its purest form is always delivered verbally in a highly pompous and deeply sincere, righteous and humorless manner. It generally has a high *sametalk* content.

gorelook = a series of smarmy "confidential" facial expressions accompanying *goretalk* designed to show that good manners and possibly the libel laws prohibit the speaker from sharing with you explicitly the terrible truth about the speaker's opponents. These include: the knowing head shake, the small secret-sharing smile, the what can-you-expect shrug. The first two *gorelooks* also are used

11

as background for positive non-verbal support of *willietalk.*

adspeak = a long-established and peculiarly American form of language pollution in which a totally or partially fictional reality is described in a highly sincere-sounding vocabulary: fantasy is presented as fact. See: *fantasyspeak.*

badguy labels = ad hominem, clearly negative words thrown at opposition when irrationality of argument becomes apparent. e.g., mean-spirited, divisive, extremist

bizschoolspeak = technical-sounding neutral words for organizational actions that often involve unpleasant results or desperate gambles. e.g., reengineering for massive firings. See: *corporatespeak.*

bravebabble = a word or phrase used to try to avoid blame and the personal consequences of an act; e.g., making much of stating that "the buck stops here."

category shift = the tactic of trying to remove from discussion and consideration a major error by moving it into a belittling or negative category -- preferably one that has been besmirched in the past. e.g., McCarthyism, extremism, a numbers game, old news.

Chinese-lunch talk = very familiar, good sounding big abstractions that please when heard but leave the mind empty of intellectual nourishment. e.g., freedom, democracy. A form of *cotton-candytalk.*

codetalk = use of superficially innocuous words or phrases to signal very significant and specific messages, often warnings, criminal or immoral activity or legal outs. See: *introcode.*

commiespeak = an entire Orwellian upside down vocabulary developed by the former Soviet Union, the Communist Party, Communist Leaders Nikolai Lenin and Joseph Stalin and their followers designed to label enemies with the label creator's worst crimes (See: imperialist warmonger) or to sugar coat outrageously those dark activities with the most positive descriptions. (See: people's republic) A special subschool of *diabolictalk.*

corporatespeak = top management glossology for all negative developments; much influenced by *bizschoolspeak*; also used to coat very simple ideas with a veneer of profundity and magic.

cotton-candytalk = clichés that have become emptied of almost all meaning and emotive power through overuse and abuse but still carry some minor ritualistic values and comfy feelings at least for the speaker. A grouping of words that have become a vacuum phrase can be easily identified when anyone who has not recently arrived by alien spacecraft can complete the sentence in advance. e.g., "We must make sure that these (victims, soldiers, workers, thoroughbred horses) have not died (_*__.)

cutespeak = self-deprecating and/or witty phraseology designed to cloak or absolve inimical intent.

cry-wolf talk = grossly inaccurate and increasing use of powerful words to make a highly negative rhetorical point, a practice resulting in marked depreciation of the power of such words. e.g., Hitler, Gestapo

diabolictalk = hyperbolic negative classification of opponents as members of an evil non-existent grouping that has taken on mythological reality. e.g., Adolf Hitler's "international Jewish conspiracy," Joseph Stalin's "capitalist imperialist warmongers", Hillary Clinton's "vast right wing conspiracy."

fantasyspeak = an advanced stage of *adspeak* in which any attempt to use factual-sounding language is abandoned because the auditor so wants to believe the fantasy is real that the need to cosmetize it is unnecessary. *Fantasyspeak* is a particularly virulent form of language pollution when both speaker and auditor want the fantasy to be real and reinforce each other. See *adspeak*.

fliptalk = conversion of once highly positive or acceptably neutral words into code words for *libtalk* negative concepts. e.g., militia, military, hunter.

gift-wrap package name (GWPN) = an attractive, fuzzy name wrapped around one or more painful raw chunks of reality; often the latest of a series of *GWPN*'s adopted successively as the previous *GWPN* wears thin. See: *leapfrogging*.

gooeytalk = nauseatingly sticky, hyper-sentimental words and phrases designed to inflate and coat with unwarranted sanctification normal and often mundane human functions and relationships. e.g., nurture for taking care of one's children; care giver for bedpan emptier, Also see closely related *pathostalk*.

governmentspeak (gobbledegook) = an argot-ridden Language of Obfuscation; an entire, always expanding vocabulary of technical-sounding, pretentious, complex neologisms and newly-defined masking words and phrases designed to baffle and confuse the citizenry while enfolding the Permanent Bureaucracy in spurious professionalism and protective mystery.

Halloweentalk = sinister, tendentious, overblown and scary implications built into once straight-forward positive words or descriptive phrases. e.g., cuts in spending.

inflator = a word or phrase – either pejorative or overly positive – replacing accurate but mundane descriptors with the intention to hype.

introcode = a special category of *codetalk* used to begin a statement with the hidden signal that what the auditor is about to read or hear is a fabrication that the faithful must believe. e.g., it is well known; so what

leapfrogging = the tactic of abandoning words and phrases

and arbitrarily jumping to new ones when the old word or phrase has become clearly noisome or totally vacuous.

libtalk = a heady brew of *gooeytalk* and the language of arrogant do-goodism that seeks to advocate or perform sanctimonious-sounding deeds and policies that do not apply or affect the do-gooder beyond assuaging guilt for elitist ambitions and often personal greed.

mister-niceguy terminology (gooeytalk) = mamby-pamby, empty words designed when sanctimoniously invoked to shift fact-based discussion to some ethereal world where anyone who questions your position is clearly in the wrong for doing just that regardless of the facts. e.g., healing process, future generations or our grandchildren, peace process, the children.

misunderstanding ploy = feel-good cover to obscure and explain changes of the rules in the middle of the game (e.g., social security), blatant opposition and rejection (e.g., Clinton Health Plan) or violent reaction (e.g., the Cold War).

negative engorgement = heavy addition of negative implications and baggage to previously neutral word or phrase. e.g. white male, Eurocentric

pagantalk = pseudo-scientific terminology from the underground of witchcraft, mythology and pagan religions along with adapted *gooeytalk* .

pathostalk = persistent over utilization of emotion-laden words or abstractions along with appropriate sighs, catches in the throat, Hollywood-moist eyes. e.g., the children, mothers, the sick, Christmas

phony badge words = descriptions that sound good or important but either have no substantive meaning, are highly inflated or both. e.g., customer service representative, sanitary engineer, care provider.

plastertalk = minor admissions of error or attempts to garner sympathy to cover up such things as major personal failures, stupidities, crimes or moral lapses. e.g., "My back was bothering me." or "Everyone makes a few mistakes."

position engorgement = heavy addition of baggage that supports a particular position or special interest; adding invisible impedimenta that makes a positive word a cause-rallying code word.

sametalk = deliberate repetitive use of a heavily freighted code word or phrase preferably by many different people in a short period of time.

spin (spinspeak) = general noun or verb for transmogrification of any word or descriptor into what sounds like a positive idea or development after all; a modern adaptation of the practice of sophistry.

technogook = technical, clean-sounding terms for unpleasant realities; particularly favored by the military, governments and the medical profession.

e.g., sympathetic detonation for setting off larger explosions with human bombs. Also used as scientific icing to obscure or inflate mundane matters.

tin-eartalk = stumblebum, awkward words and phrases put together as euphemisms to achieve political correctness or elitist "simplification" for the intellectual unwashed. This approach leads to such abominations as the rewriting of The Lord's Prayer.

Trojan-horse construction = A word or phrase that pre-labels you as being in the wrong if you refuse to go along with whatever outrages and fallacious assumptions are inside the horse's skin.

world-endtalk = use of words or phrases that imply that the Vandals are at the gates and the looting and raping is about to begin.

vacuumtalk = once viable expressions now emptied of substance by repeated abuse. See: *cotton-candytalk*

Language Pollution Dictionary

Language pollution today is increasingly dynamic. No sooner do lexicographers strip away a layer of pollution to reveal hard-rock, real meaning than another layer is applied. All of the definitions provided here in the *Language Pollution Dictionary* expose current pollution of words and phrases all of which are subject to possible further mutation and pollution at any time. To understand this process, keep in mind that the basic objective of all language pollution: the selling of snake oil as nectar.

A.

abuse = non-eradicable psychic and/or physical wounding beginning normally at birth or earlier that explains away even the most outrageous anti-social behavior throughout an individual's life. (See: victim)

according to my legal counsel = my lawyer says that what I did was not illegal so don't blame me if it was. See: no controlling legal authority.

activist = a positive descriptor of a special interest group or person favoring your position and probably benefiting from it.; a negative descriptor of an interest group or person favoring a position that you oppose Formerly strictly unpaid, but increasingly involved with personal material gain. (See: special interest and citizens groups).

adult correctional institution = prison

advocate = *phony badge word* upgrade for customer care representative and customer service as both terms have become obviously meaningless.

ADL = *gobbledegook* acronym for "Activities of Daily Living" which is Medicare *gobbledegook* for referring in pseudoscientific toney manner to such tasks as brushing your teeth, tying your shoes and eating your soup.

adversative = *spinspeak* for tough military school hazing scrubbed up with a new label after court-ordered admission of women.

affinity room = a room in a library where members of a designated group can go and read about themselves. e.g., Rooms for homosexuals, blacks, South Sea islanders, Inuits. No rooms are known to have been set up for Americans of German, French, Italian or Japanese ancestry.

affirmative action = *libtalk* for development of quota systems that promote designated losers.

age appropriate = public school educational *technogook* for a student who does not cause trouble and can see lightening and hear thunder.

agency = *governmentspeak neo*-verb meaning to give something normally earned to those who have not done so. (See: empower, disadvantaged) age appropriate behavior = the level of behavior in public school at which one has to demonstrate failure in order to receive Social Security (SSI) disability payments; such payments often based on parent-encouraged performance are known as crazy money in the welfare constituency.

aggressive = *badguy label* for anyone competently doing his job in disclosing outrageous and/or criminal conduct. See: goes too far.

aggressive accounting = *corporatespeak* for simmering—as opposed to cooking—the books.

air campaign = Pentagon *spinspeak* for systematic bombing subsequently embraced and expanded by former doves as *willietalk* for no-casualty war preferably all conducted at a very great distance. See: phased air campaign.

alone = potentially compromising condition that can be denied with the *willietalk* phrase "not alone together" if you leave the door open a crack e.g. *There were a lot of times when we were alone but I never really thought we were...It depends how you define alone.* (President Clinton grand jury testimony.)

all about = a generally fallacious and usually all but empty omnibus phrase that pretentiously implies great wisdom as in "democracy (happiness, education) is what this program is all about." A variety of *Chinese-lunch talk.*

alternative lifestyle = uni-gender marriage, cross dressing, pederasty. See: alternate sexual preference, sexual preference, sexual orientation.

alternate sexual preference = sexual deviance, sodomy, whips and chains; shortened by most to simply sexual preference since alternate is clearly implied.

alternative turkey = a non-meat turkey for vegetarians who otherwise might feel like outsiders on Thanksgiving. Alternative turkeys are made of tofu (the "Tofurky") or wheat gluten (the "UnTurkey" from a company called Now and Zen of San Francisco.)

American dream = the highly energizing possibility of upward mobility which (despite all evidence to the contrary) is no longer achievable because of the rich; of course, achieving the American dream puts you in the odious ranks of the rich, a contradiction best not pursued. See: the rich and lottery of life; synonym: middle-class dream.

anti-China crowd = *badguy label* adopted by the Clinton White House to describe anyone who finds troublesome the theft of military secrets by the Chinese Communists or the trading of military technology for campaign contributions from Chinese intelligence agents.

angry white males = pejorative description for white men (and women) [See: *spin*] disturbed by affirmative action that favors minority group members over them; terminology carries implications of insensitive red-neck Neanderthals.

appearance problem = *willietalk* for explaining why you are not a duck (or, more to the point, an immoral sleaze and/or a crook) just because you walk and talk like one. See: mistakes, lapses in judgment.

apology = *vacuumtalk figleaf* that shows how compassionate you are and makes everything OK but involves no personal penalty or inconvenience; much used to gain public admiration in connection with long past evils with which the apologizer had no connection such as slavery, the Inquisition, the Holocaust and suppression of the Huguenots. See: buck stops here; take responsibility. Also see: contrition.

astrology = a science that has much to say to the world's victims and searchers. (See: victim, searcher.)

attention deficiency syndrome (ADS) = borrowed *psychobabble* phrase used to explain persistence of bad schools and justify large demands for special education spending and government disability handouts.

B.

balance = negative information about an opponent whether it exists or not that you call for in response to hearing negative facts about yourself.

based on what I know = *introcode* intended to justify to the unwary an affirmative statement that more than likely will prove to be completely fallacious. e.g., President Clinton: "Based on what I know today, I have confidence in the way the Justice Department is handling it."

better communications = what is needed when programs are rejected on their merits. e.g., Hillary Clinton (post major defeats in 1994 congressional elections): "We failed to articulate the vision."

bewildered = *willietalk* sugarcoating denial of an accusation carrying a high probability of being true. Polluted synonyms: shocked, mystified. (See)

beyond civil discourse = *willietalk* pejorative label used to put down criticism stated in unambiguous language often employing Anglo-Saxon words.

beyond politics (also beyond partisanship) = *willietalk* for stigmatizing opposition proposals as being purely political in motivation as compared to Administration proposals which are by implication non-partisan acts of leadership.

billing partner = *codetalk* for unindicted coconspirator first used in this sense to refer to First Lady Hillary Clinton.

bipartisan = the good behavior that you exhibit when you go along with Democratic liberal positions; no bipartisanship is the other guy's position when not in agreement with the person speaking. See: consensus, partisan and put politics aside.

birth mother = *libtalk technogook* for a female who gives birth to a child; gives the child up for adoption, and irresponsibly allows herself to be "discovered" years later to the probable financial betterment of the psychiatric community. See: biological parent.

bi-lingual education = primarily bad Spanish, no English; limited or no reading capability in either.

biological parent = *libtalk technogook* for father or mother before sperms and eggs were donated or purchased from strangers. See: birth mother.

boorish = *plastertalk* to describe outrageous and totally unacceptable conduct. Used as a descriptor in the famous federal court decision summarily dismissing charges as not a legal offense that President Clinton groped a woman, then dropped his trousers and requested fellatio. See: bumptious.

bridge = *position engorgement* for a Wizard of Oz yellow brick road going to a magical land as in the "bridge to the 21st Century" promised by the Clinton

Administration.

brutally honest = *willietalk* cover for obfuscation.

buck stops here = famous Trumanism for real acceptance of responsibility and continued endorsement of the positions involved; now *vacuumtalk* for: "I'll be brave and say it was my fault, but gosh, we're only human; no one really did it, and, even if *they* did, it was all just a mistake, I'm sure." See: responsibility.

build down = *willietalk* for unilateral disarmament by an enemy

bumptious = *plastertalk* used by White House to describe presidential conduct that included groping a female employee, dropping of presidential trousers and a request for fellatio. See: boorish.

bureaucratic snafu = *figleaf* -- particularly government *figleaf* -- for wrong-doing ranging from moral outrage to criminal activity. See: honest mistake.

bystanders = *spinspeak* discounting of people not categorized as part of a minority group who are adversely affected when affirmative action programs are used to benefit minority group members; e.g., white men.

care provider = downward equalizing *gooeytalk* for doctors, nurses, medical aides; also mothers, fathers, brothers, sisters, aunts, uncles, cousins, neighbors; also the growing quasi-professional army of care workers (See: care workers).

care workers = permanent employees and related polyps of the Welfare Industry.

caring = typical 60's gooey-talk word for self-fulfilling and potentially remunerative meddling with the lives of the lower classes.

censure = near *vacuumtalk* for insincere and cynically generated criticism embraced to shield against an oncoming bullet.

children = pathos-talk word usually invoked with a catch in the throat and suddenly moist eyes. e.g., spending cuts that would deprive children of (fill in blank); often employed in the French language universal: *the children* implying all children in the universe thereby elevating compassion to the global level.

children of (unwed) single parents = bastards

challenged = handicapped, abnormal. e.g., a dwarf is vertically challenged. See: impaired, otherabled change = positive descriptor of whatever you want to do or have been doing and have now repackaged; carries implication of popular demand.

charges against restructuring = *corporatespeak* for a sewer pipe through which all management error no matter how egregious can be flushed without penalty.

child care = *willietalk* substitute for day care when the latter took on the nuance of abuse by selfish women who delegate motherhood to strangers.

choice = ostensibly what women (and men) would like to have about most things but now a position engorged word meaning women have a right to choose whether to abort their children; moreover, the choice of choice is generally abortion. All abortion clinics are pro-choice. Women favoring alternatives to abortion generally are for choosing right to life rather than choice. See: reproductive rights.

citizens group = a special interest group that favors and usually will benefit from your position.

client = professional welfare recipient required to maintain the Welfare Industry. (See: the poor.)

collateral damage = military *spinspeak* for near-miss bombing that results in blowing up homes, shopping centers and aspirin factories and killing a lot of civilians – formerly the wildly popular "bring home the war" targets of American, British, German and Japanese bombers in World War II.

common ground = *willietalk* for where everyone comes together after you alone have handed over your sword. (See: vital center)

communications = public relations, *spin* (See: better)

community outreach meeting = *willietalk* for illegal fund-raising activity.. See: donor maintenance. Language pollution popularized by Vice President Gore in explaining his political fund raising at a Buddhist Shrine.

companion animal = pet (generic for dogs, cats, birds, fish, turtles, ferrets, gerbils); *willietalk* avoiding the esteem-destroying connotation of one species owning another.

complainant = mugged, beaten, raped or murdered citizen.

compassionate = enormously exaggerated gooey feelings by elitists for the less fortunate members of society usually in indirect ratio to proximity; lack of compassion = mean-spiritedness, hateful (See:).

compassionate imperialism = See: liberal colonialism.

complicating factor = *willietalk* for disastrous turn of events often exposing an underlying lack of substance.

comprehensive review = Second line of defense *willietalk* for rather than the real action proposed we will look at it for a long time.

congenital disability = birth defect such a being a Mongoloid or being born without hands and feet. See: challenged and impaired.

consensus = the positive nirvana that is achieved when opposition to your unchanged position ceases (See: bipartisan)

conspiracy = *willietalk* slander of what the opposition is doing even though there is obviously nothing secret or illegal about it and thereby eroding the old definition of conspiracy: secret plotting to commit illegal acts. See: *diabolictalk,* vast right wing conspiracy.

constructive engagement = all carrot, no stick. (See: strategic ambiguity)

content = *adspeak technogook* for the rather basic though not universally held thought that communications (e.g., books, plays, TV movies, websites) no matter how glitzy ought to have some substance.

contributions = taxes

contrition = *vacuumtalk* employed by the obviously uncontrite for "I am truly sorry that I was caught." See: apology

conventional weapons = Pentagon and dove *spinspeak* for any non-nuclear or non-chemical weapon no matter how devastating; the implication is the war will be fought with dull spears and rubber-tipped arrows.

counterrevolutionary vermin = Stalinist *commiespeak* for Old Bolsheviks who were or whom Stalin thought were opposed Stalin's policies.

corrective labor = reform of political dissidents in the former Communist Soviet Union under the infamous GULAG (chief administration of corrective labor camps or Glavnoe Upravlenie ispravitel'-no-trudovykh LAGerei). In Communist China the Chinese named the similar corrective labor program *laogai* (reform through labor). See: reeducation.

crisis = *cry-wolf talk* word much loved and much vitiated through indiscriminate usage by 24-hour TV cable news producers to describe most on-going news stories.

crazy money = politically incorrect nomenclature used by welfare recipients of federal government disability payments (Supplemental Security Income or SSI) for their children's learning disability which they achieve through demonstrating lack of age appropriate behavior. (See) Also called crazy checks and dummy dollars. The SSI program was originally created in 1972 to aid poor adults too old, ill or disabled to work.

crowdpleaser = Pentagon *cutespeak* name for the B-53 "citybuster," a 9 megaton nuclear bomb reported to be the largest in the U.S. arsenal in the late '90s.

customer care = commercial *inflator* used as a noun or adjective to suggest even as you are being abused, inconvenienced, cheated or all three that you are "really important" to this company and someone upstairs is thinking about you.

courtesy call = *adspeak* for an intrusive, irritating sales phone call usually made at dinnertime or later in the evening by an ill-informed, illiterate "telemarketer" reading haltingly from a disingenuous script.

customer relations = a closed-loop multi-menu automatic answering service that after 10 to 15 minutes of asking irrelevant questions may provide an additional musical interlude with promotional messages with the dubious promise that a customer relations representative (See:) "is serving other customers" but will be with you as soon as possible.

customer relations representative = in most cases an affirmative action (See:) employee who only has a first name such as Wanda, Tina or Elvira, can not spell "customer" and is righteously annoyed that you are calling.

customer satisfaction = a highly desirable condition advocated by management consultants and believed to exist much of the time only by top corporate executives and advertising copywriters.

customer service = a badge word usually containing little substance designed to dispose of customer questions and complaints as swiftly and cheaply as possible. Customer service is often dispensed by a customer care representative who really doesn't.

cut = *fliptalk* used to attack any effort no matter how appropriate to slow growth of enormous planned increases in government spending deadbeat dads = originally conceived as a cute pejorative designed to embarrass middle-class divorced fathers who cheat on providing child-support but, in reality, incorporates an army of irresponsible low-lifes including particularly cokehead and/or jailbird AWOL non-supporting biological fathers of illegitimate children by teenage moms (See).

death penalty = a barbaric form of punishment usually inflicted on socially-impaired blacks who commit unspeakable crimes only because they suffer from social impairment.

deathing room = happy talk for death chamber developed by practitioners of the grief counseling dodge seeking to make a growing client population of non-religious elderly citizens and their relatives comfy with last things.

deep background = information provided the media on agreement that it will neither be attributed to the source or the source's organization, i.e., neither the President or "White House sources." Under normal accepted media rules, information provided under a background agreement can quote sources in the source's organization; off the record information is never supposed to be attributed. See: psych background

deconstruction = political rewriting of history to position
    the losers as the winners.

defining moment = heavy breathing pop history phrase used
    to hype the importance of relatively unimportant
    events; particularly events that advance various
    political attitudes, popular nostrums and herd
    thinking in general. Draws rapidly decreasing
    credibility from its original meaning: a rare dramatic
    event that in the long view truly marked a
    momentous change in the world. e.g., The
    Crucifixion or some lesser matter such as the
    beginning of World War I.

degrade = military *spinspeak* enabling politicians to
    establish with considerable fanfare fudgey bombing
    objectives that could in reality range anywhere from
    total obliteration of an unused garage to significant
    but reparable damage to a radar site.

delayering = *bizschoolspeak* for organizational restructuring
    primarily involved with firing middle management.
    See: reengineering.

de facto recusal = remaining in position to influence events
    but promising not to do that.

deliberate force = *gift-package wrap* name adopted to take
    the place of discredited measured response used in
    the Viet Nam War to describe slowly escalating
    levels of military power; good example of
    leapfrogging

delinquent = juvenile criminal predator; note delinquent,

itself, has been displaced by societal victim.

Democratic Party of the Left = *leapfrogging* title for the Communist Party in Italy (*Partito Democraticico della Sinistra*) after the collapse of the Communist Soviet Union and the bankruptcy of its economic and political system.

deprived = lacking something with the clear implication that someone else is keeping it from you. e.g., the reason you do not look like a movie star, add like Einstein and sing like Pavoratti is the result of social deprivation not eight generations of bad genes. See: challenged, impaired.

deterrent capacity = a preponderance of arms sufficient to make an opponent tread softly.

difference feminism = women should run the world because they basically are cuddly, caring non-competitive marshmallows who prefer to cooperate rather than compete unlike their hateful chauvinist male counterparts.

D&E (dilation and extraction) = *libtalk technogook* for partial birth abortion, a medical procedure involving the killing of a fully-formed fetus while only the head is still inside its mother's body.

disadvantaged = any situation of comparative difference with the implication that redress is both needed and morally required. See: deprived and victim disappointing = *spinspeak* adjective for describing criminal and/or grossly immoral activity.

discomfort = *medispeak* for intense pain; readily adopted and incorporated into current *spinspeak.*

disinfection = elimination of the "unfit" in Nazi Germany. See: resettlement.

distasteful personal conduct = *willietalk* descriptor implying, for example, that self-gratification with a cigar during a sexual romp in the Oval Office while world leaders await outside ranks with blowing one's nose in a damask tablecloth at a State dinner. See inappropriate behavior, unwelcome overture and disappointing.

divisive = *badguy label* for anyone who argues with your position, particularly for those who argue rationally and successfully.

dignity of the office = *willietalk* for a traduced institution which the Chief Traducer seeks to uphold.

diversity = preference for everyone except white males. See: equal opportunity.

donor maintenance = *willietalk* descriptor for lunch attended by political contributors who paid up in advance to obtain political access through attending the lunch at which fund raising was never discussed because that had already been accomplished. See: community outreach.

dominant culture (the) = sneering pejorative for Western Civilization as compared, for example, to African culture: the purported real source, according to a number of revisionist historians, of math, science, philosophy and the Industrial Revolution among other stellar accomplishments.

downsizing = organizational restructuring usually performed in times of deep trouble. Displaced by rightsizing. See: restructuring, reengineering.

drug problem = *plastertalk* for cokehead; seeks to purvey the idea of an excessive use of aspirin.

dummy dollars = See: crazy money.

earned income = in economic terms, what Big Government regards along certainly with all unearned income as "the available"

ebonics = black illiterate street English allegedly based according to some liberal academics on "Niger-Congo idioms." e.g., the use of the words "ho's" and "bitchas" for women and "mothaf--kah" as a modest term of disrespect.

economic justice = government redistribution of assets. e.g. Cartoonist Al Capp: "We got nottin'; you got lots; we gonna share in equal pots." (See: social justice)

empower = *libtalk* for the act of arbitrarily giving vaguely defined political and economic power to someone or some group that has proven itself incapable of acquiring it. Unstated condition of the grant: the power is to be used only over people other than the givers.

encounter = *plastertalk* for salacious relationship which, in turn, was a euphemism developed during Clinton's impeachment trial for serial fellatio.

encouraged = vacuous *slickism* intended to put a positive spin on a blatantly negative or dead-in-the-water situation.

entitlement = originally the right to money that you or your heirs earned through contributions (pensions, social security) or service (military duty particularly in wartime); subsequently a broad list of unearned and increasingly dubious welfare payments authorized by law. See: guarantee.

equal opportunity = access for the most part regardless of talent to anyone except a white male. See: diversity, look like America.

establishment (the) = intended put-down reference to Western Civilization. See: (the) dominant culture, mainstream.

estate taxes = a "fair" confiscatory third or fourth bite of the apple levied on the rich beginning with the middle class who worked to achieve the American dream and at least to some degree did. (See: the rich, middle class, American dream)

equity feminism = *technogook* for a woman trampling on the rights of everyone

ethnic cleansing = fairly well-blown euphemism for forced brutal removal or killing of ethnic or religious minorities.

ethnic diversity = primarily black and Hispanic but can include any other ethnic background except European white (See: look like America)

ethnic language competence = incapacity to speak English

Eurocentric = negatively engorged word that has come to mean the total culture of dead white European males. These are the historic villains who are obviously responsible for most if not all of the misery and problems of the world particularly as opposed to the long line of accomplishments of Africans and Amerindians from whom they stole most good ideas.

evasive = *willietalk* for lying when called; usually modified with words such as "somewhat" or "a little."

event = downplaying descriptor of a major battle, atrocity or surrender designed to minimize embarrassment to the former enemy (particularly to the Japanese at the time of the 50th anniversary of the end of World War II). e.g., the events at Pearl Harbor and Bataan that lead to the events at Iwo Jima and Hiroshima that lead to the event in Tokyo Bay.

everyone (everybody) does it = *wilietalk* free pass phrase meaning that it is OK to commit whatever moral, ethical or criminal outrage is under discussion because it is suggested to be common practice and an accepted peccadillo. . See: so what.

exit strategy = overblown *technogook* for escape hatch or bug out plan; synonym for strategic withdrawal.

excessive = *inflator* for "more than I want to do;" See: way beyond and extreme.

exculpatory fellatio = *wilietalk* legalism explaining why President Clinton did not commit perjury when he denied having sexual relations with an assortment of women.

exculpatory fiction = *spinspeak* for a blatant lie used to try to explain away as a minor transgression the performance of criminal or immoral acts.

experiment with = social *technogook* used to gussy up and excuse as merely a temporary lark the admission of previous and often extensive period of smoking marijuana, "tripping" with LSD, snorting cocaine, popping a cornucopia of "funny" pills.

expropriation = Bolshevik Russian for robbing banks and wealthy individuals to finance terrorism: bomb factories and unemployed terrorists .

extra large = *adspeak* for the size something used to be before the cost cutters got to it. *adspeak* synonyms: jumbo size, king size

extreme = any proposal that threatens significant reduction in government spending, tax relief or reduction in size of government. Such proposals are made, of course, by extremists.

extremists = *badguy label* developed by the Clinton Administration for anyone opposing the programs of the Great Society. Association with usually accepted meaning (bomb-throwing anarchist killer) not denied. See: extreme.

facilitator = *willietalk* for pimp, popularized in the Clinton Administration to euphemistically describe the presidential procurement activities of Secret Service agents and, previously in Arkansas, State Troopers.

fair = *cottoncandy* label for whatever nostrum is being peddled.

fair share = money stolen by the government in taxes from those who work for it to give to those who don't but do vote.

falling into poverty = liberal code *Halloweentalk* for imminent impoverishment of the middle class

family values = *cotton-candytalk* for living based on the Ten Commandments with numerous loopholes and snake oil exceptions depending on the speaker. See: rules.

farm fresh = not necessarily very old. See: fresh frozen

feel good = often feel good about yourself, a euphoric state that somehow can be delivered through compassionate government programs as opposed to mean-spirited realistic self-help approaches. See: compassionate, mean-spirited

fending for yourself = economic abandonment of the

individual by liberal Big Government, a *willietalk* negative *spin* on the 400-year American concept self-help, individualism and the frontier.

fertility regulation = family planning that invariably includes abortion

fighting squads = Bolshevik Communist terrorist cells. See: expropriation.

first step = *bravebabble* used to coverup inadequacy or total failure of the result of a negotiation or effort much touted in advance; particularly favored by foreign policy officials following major diplomatic meetings.

follow the rules (those who) = w*illietalk* code phrase for what used to be called "the little guy" (now considered mean spirited language), all the hard-working, moral, honest folk who always do the right thing and seem always to get the short end of the stick (and, therefore, need government help just like *the poor* (See) as opposed to *the rich* (See). As a pragmatic matter, the government will as always obtain most of the money to give things to hard-workers who follow the rules from the same hard-workers who follow the rules because they are the ones who have the bulk of it.

force protection = military *gobbledegook* for conducting no-casualties bloodless war: rather than seeking the classic military doctrine of seeking to achieve victory in battle with as few casualties as possible. The force protection doctrine employs military technology to achieve limited objectives well short of victory but still calls it that.

forensic evidence = technogook used in the Clinton White House scandals as a euphemism for presidential semen.

free elections = any voting no matter how corrupted as long as it is "observed" by UN observers and/or former President Jimmy Carter.

freedom = a Nirvana-like political condition that endows all citizens (and non-citizens) with an inalienable right without penalty to ignore the Ten Commandments and other wet blanket ideas should they choose to do so.

freedom fighters = thugs or terrorists on your side often with questionable yearnings for somewhat less than freedom for others. See: terrorist.

fresh frozen = usually chickens or fish that were not dead very long when they were frozen at some earlier time, but bear in mind that woolly mammoths were fresh frozen. See: farm fresh.

from my point of view = *codetalk* phrase preceding or following some spin designed to talk away an outrage or worse. The objective of the *codetalk* is to provide a legal-wiggle back-out route and, accordingly, should serve as a warning to the wary auditor.

fudge = *willietalk* verb stated as a perfectly acceptable justification for skirting announced policy or the law.

full responsibility (take) = *bravebabble* used to try to escape blame without personal penalty while absolving underlings who did what they were told. See: make mistakes, apology, buck stops here

fungible nuance = *willietalk* explanation for the rubbery description of a government patronage job given to someone to ensure happiness, forgetfulness or both.

funk = a peculiarly American pathology that according to President Clinton manifests itself in the election of Republicans; what President Carter called malaise

G.

gaming = gambling

gay = wonderful old poetic word now mutated and tattered in the mire of its sad usage as a euphemism for homosexual and less flattering words such as fag, queer and sissy.

gender norming = radical feminist-generated technogook for juggling standards enabling women to score as high as men in physical requirements for military service, police work, fire fighting and other occupations where raw physical strength can be a life or death matter.

gender perspective = *spin* word favored by radical feminist groups defining sex as socially constructed as opposed to what for some time has been called boys and girls; concept accepts numerous categories other than male and female but specifically downplays something called "mothers" and "fathers."

genocide = increasingly *diabolictalk* through inflated and inaccurate usage. See: war crimes.

Gestapo = *cry-wolftalk* term of opprobrium used rhetorically by liberals to slander opponents who choose to fight back rather than roll over; term much depreciated by incorrect usage except among the historically uneducated. (See: Hitler).

goes too far = *willietalk* description of something strongly opposed but politically necessary to pretend to embrace. See: overreaching

good girl = *willietalk* for conniving, immoral air-head.

graceful duck = artful lying

graduated income tax = the more you make the greater percentage of your pie you give to the government to skim and then pass along to its constituents; much praised by the governing liberal elite as a way to make the rich pay their fair share.

Great Society = a supposedly wonderful world of justice, happiness and goodness that in reality involves the redistribution of income by an elitist governing class from workers to a growing class of non-workers.

gridlock = what the opposition is doing when it prevents its opposition from doing something; unpatriotic tactics to thwart ultimate right thinking and good government. Or, as first popularized with a positive *spin* in the 1980's by the "good" Democratic Congress to describe what the GOP Reagan and Bush Administrations forced it to do to block "bad" GOP policies. See: politics of gridlock.

grief counseling = political liberal *psychobabble* descriptor of what politicians and others of whom they approve are doing when they look somber and teary for the TV cameras while mingling with the real mourners at funereal events. See: Grief Industry.

Grief Industry = growing army of *psycobabblers* who inflict themselves on real victims (See) of some tragedy and their friends, relatives and associates to cure vague neurosis from which the grief practitioners say they suffer.

group residency programs = orphanages

guarantee = *willietalk* for entitlement which has undergone *negative engorgement*.

guide = *gooeytalk* for discipline, possibly even punish (mildly).

H.

handfasting = *pagantalk* for a pagan marriage.

hardworking middle-class = fuzzy talk for what used to be called blue collar workers while providing a meaningless upgrade that flatters the former while trying to woo the real middle-class.

hate = an emotion you are criticized for entertaining when your money has been taken by the government to support waste and featherbedding, your property has been stolen, your neighborhood has been trashed and you fear for your life on streets crowded with convicted but protected felons and sociopaths; also a blanket condemnation of variance from new liberal political correctness. e.g., hate talk, hate thinking, hate ideas, hate crime.

hateful = use of irony, satire or sarcasm to demonstrate truth while engendering ridicule of abuses and laughter; e.g., much of the writing of H.L. Mencken, Mark Twain and Jonathan Swift is clearly hateful.

haves = pejorative synonym for the rich (See) – the greedy people who clip coupons and who should always pay more taxes – as opposed to the have nots who in this comparison are the middle class and the poor but in reality only the welfare-dependent classes; in reality to pay for the Great Society the haves must include the middle class for tax purposes and wealth

50

redistribution..

have nots = See: haves.

healing = *gooey*talk word used to fend off reform and denigrate opposition; hidden agenda is that healing will result in improvement of the user's position even if it is nothing but a placebo.

healing consultant = *technogook* spawn of psychobabble sent into a disaster situation with much fanfare in lieu of more costly real help. See: grief counseling.

healing process = *Mister-niceguy* terminology called for to paper over real disagreement on an issue or embarrassing occurrence and to brand anyone seeking to continue the argument as an obvious troublemaker. (See: process.) "Let the healing begin" = "Let's change the subject."

heed = *fuzzy talk* for obey.

heterosexual = *negatively engorged* to mean only one -- and probably not the best -- sexual alternatives available except for those blindly intent on survival of the mankind. See: humankind.

high crimes and misdemeanors = a monumentally high level of evil criminal conduct that according to liberal apologists and their self-serving running dogs can be risen to only by Republicans.

high-quality = *adspeak* for something that, no kidding. is really better than average and, therefore, needs to be distinguished from a quality product or service that is really only average.

Hiroshima = *libtalk* icon for a large Japanese city mostly occupied almost entirely by peace-loving women and beautiful happy children obliterated unnecessarily by vengeful American imperialists with an atomic bomb in connection with some vague altercation over cultural differences. See: War in the Pacific.

his and/or her = an awkward, tin-ear euphemism for the generic use of "his" in sentences such as: "Everyone is responsible for keeping his room clean."

Hispanic = Various ethnic mixtures (blacks, Indians, possibly some early Spaniards) from Latin America. Pureblooded Spaniards from Spain and often Latin America not included. Also: "the Hispanic language" which presumably is some version of Spanish.

Hitler = *cry-wolftalk* term of opprobrium used with outrageous historical inaccuracy by liberal politicians and their camp followers to describe opponents; meaning much depreciated by such usage. (See: Gestapo).

homeless = *gooeytalk* for professional street beggar, alcoholic/drug addict, wastrel, deinstitutionalized mental case; *negative engorgement* of a word originally identifying the condition of someone temporarily down on his luck often because of natural disasters such as floods.

Homeless cosmopolitans = *commiespeak* used in the Stalinist purge of 1949 to describe intelligentsia (mostly Jewish) allegedly guilty of "kowtowing to the West...and things foreign." (It was during this period that Stalinist historians discovered that Russians had invented the light bulb, airplane, radio and many other technical achievements -- all stolen by Western foreigners.)

honest mistake = *figleaf* form of *plastertalk* for a variety of outrages, ethical and moral lapses and criminal activities. See: bureaucratic snafu, mistakes were made.

ho's = generic illiterate *gangsta rap* word for women; sometimes combined in the phrase "ho's and bitchas." See: ebonics.

hospitality = making guest rooms in the private quarters of the White House available to large political donors.

hostile environment = *libtalk* for justifying self-satisfying elitist suppression of freedom of speech in order to obtain a social environment that denies human behavior.

Human One = Son of Man (from an inclusive edition of The New Testament, Oxford University Press, 1995); same inclusive rewrite substitutes Teacher for Master; God the Father-Mother for God the Father or Our Father and Dominion of God for Kingdom of God; mighty hand for right hand; eliminates "dark" and "darkness" as representing evil.

humankind = a tin-ear "sensitive" substitute for "mankind"
or simply Man as in "Man is the measure of all
things." See: his and/or her.

hunter = gun-loving militaristic, Neanderthal who
indiscriminately kills animals and birds preferably
with large calibre assault weapons. See: military.

I.

I do not recall = probable legal dodge to avoid taking the
Fifth Amendment when questioned under oath. Part
of a family of such legal *willietalk* such as: I do not
remember; I do not have a clear memory of that; I
don't have any direct knowledge; I am not aware; To
my knowledge, no; To the best of my memory.

I will answer as accurately as I can = *willietalk* for "My
check is in the mail."

identified = politically preapproved regardless of
subsequent examination and investigation, as in
identified candidate for a position.

if true = a *spin* conditional interjected as much as possible
in a very weak case to suggest that after all maybe
what everyone thinks is true may not be after all.
See: rush to judgment.

impaired = abnormal, inadequate. e.g., people who eat
without benefit of knives and forks; spray paint
buildings, or engage in freeform rape and pillage are
socially impaired -- a condition, therefore, best dealt
with by the Poverty Industry workers rather than
firing squads. (now generally dropped in favor of
challenged because of its negative overtones.) See:
otherabled and challenged.

imperialist warmonger = *commiespeak* epithet for any

individual or nation opposed to the Soviet Union's drive for world hegemony.

impose peace = dovish *spinspeak* for use of bombing to execute the ancient Roman strategy of pacification through the creation of a desert.

improper = *willietalk* for undefined bad acts not performed by the speaker, particularly not performed by members of the Clinton Administration; often employed in blanket denials such as "I did nothing improper."

inappropriate behavior = *willietalk* for sexual hanky-panky that some spoilsports might consider improper, e.g., serial fellatio in the Oval Office provided President Clinton by a 21-year old White House intern. This phraseology is particularly applicable when the intern is in action while the President is talking on the phone to a prominent congressman. See: sexual relations (deniable); *plastertalk* that implies whatever happened was similar to a failure to use the correct fork or even so bad as failing to wash one's hands before eating.

inappropriate laughter = *libtalk* hate crime definition for finding amusing the contorted language used by the gurus of political correctness -- particularly in the Temples of Academe -- to justify the failings of their client Victim Community.

inappropriate sexual banter = *willietalk* for phone sex which some blue noses would define as explicit sexual conversation accompanied by what in a more delicate age was called self-abuse.

independent state grounds = *gobbledegook* of the liberal judiciary for tortured interpretations of the often sloppy wording in state constitutions to favor such pet constituencies as homosexuals, sociopaths down on their luck, illegal immigrants and select minority groups in violation of the rights of all citizens under the U.S. Constitution -- particularly rights previously upheld by the U.S. Supreme Court.

in-depth language = *commiespeak* for a statement bearing coded meaning that the auditor is expected to understand and on which he is expected to act. e.g., private statements by Stalin to his closest associates that it would be best for them to commit suicide rather than going through the messy business of confessing to trumped up charges for the good of the Party, being brought to trial and executed.

inclusion = the right of anyone, absolutely anyone, to join the party as in "never mind about bathing, just go right in." See: inclusive.

inclusive = everyone is welcome and equal (and, if not, we'll work on it) in the great bouillabaisse of life (except, of course, for us chefs); or, big square pegs can be made to fit into little round holes after all.

income inequality = a *Trojan horse construction* for economic state based on the underlying belief that it is basically unfair that somehow people who work have more income than people who don't and this situation should be corrected by punitive taxes and payouts by the government bureaucrats.

individualism = a popular form of behavior that entitles an individual to freedom to do whatever he wishes regardless of how offensive or damaging it might be to his neighbors. See: freedom.

Indigenous Peoples Day = Columbus Day. (Supporters of this change contend that Columbus and his Spanish associates treated viciously indigenous people such as the Aztecs and obliterated their quaint folkways; e.g. human sacrifice by ripping out the hearts of live victims and the thrifty use of the remains as an important protein supplement.)

investment = spending of public money; usually pork. See: strategic investment.

irrational exuberance = dangerous run away speculation in the stock market; phrase first used by Federal Reserve Chairman Alan Greenspan in December 1996 resulting in an immediate drop in the market; recanted by him the following April and the return of bullish conditions.

is = *willietalk* use of the present tense of the verb to be to imply exclusion of the past. As explained by President Clinton to a grand jury: *It depends on what the meaning of the word "is" is.*

it is well known = *commiespeak introcode* for stating an outrageous official fiction that is to be accepted immediately as gospel by all auditors should they wish to remain in this world.

Ivan Vasilievich = Signature recognized by Soviet intelligence officers on secret encoded telegrams from Soviet Leader Josef Stalin aka Koba aka Josef Dzhugashvili: originally it was the Christian name and patronymic of Czar Ivan the Terrible.

job training = government training program usually unrelated to market demand or worker capability.

journey = *willietalk* for a lengthy period of public wiggling and quasi-denial of disgraceful behavior claimed to be a good moral lesson for the children.

just = *introcode* for assuming protective off-handedness for a major and clearly controversial statement, accusation or admission.. e.g., "I just wanted you to know that he took the money."

just a few = *willietalk* phrase for minimizing a rash of blatantly illegal or unethical acts or incidents.

justice = *spinspeak* usage for describing the giving a pass to the clearly guilty for social or genetic reasons.

L.

lack of due discretion = *gobbledegook* grounds for annulment of long-time fully consummated marriages of the political class.

lapses in judgment = *willietalk* for "mistakes were made" or "appearance problem" to describe a plethora of outrages and criminal activities. See both; also see: inappropriate behavior.

law guardian = court-appointed defense lawyer for a juvenile who more likely than not will succeed in further undermining law and order by springing the cold-hearted little felon as quickly as possible.

leadership = *cotton-candytalk* for whatever the speaker happens to propose.

lean and mean = *corporatespeak* for downsizing (See) and often an array of showy but small change economies that normally will not impinge on top management.

learning disability = easily feigned ephemeral malady highly useful in obtaining government welfare as well as other special benefits such as unfair advantage in taking scholastic exams See: crazy money.

leave = *willietalk* rubber-word originally used in the sense of exiling a military dictator but subsequently to mean anything from leave power to briefly leave the room.

lebensborn = Nazi German "fountain of life" maternity homes established in the 1930s for unwed mothers and social experiments aimed at breeding super citizens, often located near racially elite SS corps camps and used as stud farms.

legally correct = *willietalk* for a blatant lie, criminal act, gross immorality or combination of all three that is claimed not to be any one of the three because of some slick legalism. See: no controlling legal authority.

legislative craftsmanship = condemnatory professional praise for opponents who were very adroit about getting their allegedly evil proposals through Congress.

(the) level of perjury = *spinspeak* high water mark non-existent in fact or law to which the felony of lies made under oath are supposed to "rise to" before they become truly perjurious for the chosen few and anything about which anyone really should worry much in these sophisticated and enlightened times.

lewinsky = euphemism for fellatio; derived from Monica Lewinsky, President Clinton's favorite White House intern; euphemism first employed by national TV journalists to identify to family audiences the alleged sexual act of which the President was seeking to deny in general terms being a frequent recipient in various parts of the White House including the Oval Office; used as both a n. (a lewinsky), a vt. (to lewinsky) and an adj. (lewinsky).

liberal = motherhood word, somewhat tattered and much changed since its intellectual glory days in the 18th Century, but still offering positive feelings for many -- particularly those deriving elitist superiority through aiding the preferably distant downtrodden and advocating leveling and the lowest common denominator for all except themselves.

lies about sex = *libtalk* seeking for chosen like-minded elites to bury through trivilization blatant lying about immoral activities that might prove embarrassing and/or incriminating. See: everybody does it, so what.

life coach = *pagantalk* for a pagan religious guru practicing touchy-feely psychotherapy probably without a license.

limited modified hangout = classic *technogook* for major trimming through use of half-truths or quarter-truths rather than outright lying -- a term and technique popularized in the Nixon Administration and widely adopted since then.

living Constitution = the view held by some Supreme Court Justices and other lesser judges and political allies that the US Constitution means not what it says but whatever it ought to mean.

liberal colonialism = colonialism when practiced by "well

meaning" liberals; a euphemism for compassionate imperialism.

liberty impaired = *UNspeak* for hostage as in "our troops in Bosnia have been denied liberty of movement; they are not hostages."

lingual impairment = illiteracy

little bit more = what the rich are asked to contribute when they are taxed; sometimes also described as a fair share.

lobbyist = increasingly negative term used to describe your opposition. (See: special interest.)

look like America = pack the group with blacks, homosexuals, women. and Hispanics with a smattering of other non-whites of non-European origin, preferably those with money. .

lottery of life = any economic comfort that you might have comes from pure luck or inheritance – a purported rationale for the "fairness" of a redistributionist tax policy.

loving couple = spin *gooeytalk* for two cohabiting homosexuals particularly when they are seeking to adopt one or more young boys.

LEP = *technogook* for a deficiency suffered by residents of the United States who speak the *lingua franca* of the United States very badly if at all. An acronym originated by educrats from the deficiency they call

Low English Proficiency, a condition that public funding criteria encourage the Education Industry to sustain as long as possible. Sufferers from LEP are LEPs.

M.

mainstream = what used to be a moderate, broad centrist position with a strong positive connotation but has become anything somewhere right of the extreme left depending on the position of the speaker; pejorative used by compassionate, politically correct liberals to describe "the dominant culture" or "establishment." (See)

mainstreaming = conversion of a noun with a positive connotation to a verb describing the liberal journalistic mandate that all stories involve a prescribed ratio of multi-racial sourcing and quotation.

make mistakes = *plastertalk* meaning "Us poor humans didn't do anything really wrong when we did all that stuff. We just made some mistakes." See: take full responsibility; mistake.

make no mistake = *vacuum talk*, usually said with a threatening frown, employed in an attempt to convince the auditor that the known trimmer speaking really means what is being said this time although common sense would significantly discount it.

making progress = *willietalk* (unless supported with verifiable factual details) to put a positive veneer on no progress. See: moving forward, encouraged.

managing trustee = a $100,000 contributor to the
Democratic Party entitled by virtue of patriotic
generosity to various levels of political access
including two meals with President Clinton and two
with Vice President Gore plus a basket of other
meetings with lesser officials. (A major advance on
a GOP "Team 100" offering that provided $100,000
contributors with one dinner with President Bush
following an economic briefing by White House
staffers.)

management movement = *corporatespeak* for wholesale
firing and voluntary departures. See: downsizing,
rightsizing

McCarthyism = *cry-wolftalk* rhetoric for opponents who
keep insisting that the king is truly without clothes
and should be investigated. See: Hitler, Gestapo. A
key attribute of *cry-wolftalk* is that its continual
exaggerated use vitiates its horsepower as a useful
epithet.

mental rehabilitation hospital = psychiatric or mental
hospital (formerly insane asylum, mad house, mad
ward, crazy house, nut house, Bedlam)

mean spirited = anyone opposed to confiscatory income
transfers; *badguy label* pioneered by Michael
Dukakis, former governor of Massachusetts and
unsuccessful Democratic candidate for President.

means testing = economic discrimination against hardworking citizens who play by the rules.

Medicare = *governmentspeak* for a wondrous but always inadequate tax-based health care insurance program of vague illegitimacy when used by the rich; in reality, a legalized Ponzi scheme that is paid for by all working citizens and is designed to turn over dispensation of health care to former motor vehicle bureau clerks and politicians. See: the rich; also Social Security.

memory = a once powerful tool of personal knowledge that now is a vast, mostly empty warehouse where, despite mighty searches, one can find little of the past and, therefore, can only beg forgiveness and move on See: move on. Also, see: remember.

message (signal) = diplomatic *spinspeak* for bold-sounding but ineffectual military threats and insufficient casualty-free missions.

middle class bill of rights = a gift wrap package name for some me-too middle class tax cuts proposed by a beleaguered President Clinton after the '94 elections.

middle class dreams = outrageous *gooeytalk* used as a cover for packages of government spending programs called investments (See: above)

middle income = a large, vaguely defined economic category usually invoked by liberal Democrats when they wish to imply that they seek to help people not on welfare.

ministering (to a troubled young woman) = *willietalk* for
sexual relations in the boss' office between the boss
and some willing underling; first attributed in sworn
testimony to First Lady Hillary Clinton explaining
what her husband the President was doing during
his frequent meetings with White House Intern
Monica Lewinsky.

misheard = explanation of what really happened when a
politician wishes to deny saying what reliable
witnesses heard said. This is a condition closely
related to loss of memory of an embarrassing or
incriminating event.

mislead = *willietalk* for admitting to a lie or almost a lie
when caught. See: mistake, contrition, evasive.

military = questionable Neanderthal profession taken up
mindless rednecks and other dangerous white males.
See: hunter.

militia = dangerous underground group off white
Neanderthal extremists plotting overthrow of the
government, deportation of Hispanics and
homosexuals and possibly the restoration of slavery.

millionaire = a wicked, self-indulgent fat cat and probable
exploiter whose money comes from inheritance,
questionable investments and a salary and bonus (if
any) based on dubious employment. (Exceptions:
political contributors and members of group that

looks like America.)

minority adolescent = juvenile black pimp drug pusher, probably black or Hispanic.

minority group = originally Jews and blacks; subsequently blacks alone; then Hispanics; then anyone who is not of white European ancestry plus all women despite that they are a majority, all homosexuals and lesbians, and disabled people unless they are white and have at least modest means. See: victim.

mission statement = *corporatespeak* for a grandiose, orotund and often wildly fictional description of what a corporation or organization is supposed to be doing to justify its existence. Such statements whether or not they have much relationship to reality are considered successful if they make people feel good.

mistake or mistakes were made = totally absolving description of immoral and criminal acts as in "We made a mistake and won't do it again." On the other hand, a terrible mistake is an action opposed by the speaker or one the speaker finds politically embarrassing. e.g., President Clinton called nuclear testing by India a "terrible mistake." (See: we; make mistakes; also, mislead.)

modalities = *goretalk* for how to do something.

momentum = *signal word* intended to indicate that things

are going along just fine even though they may not be; e.g. "We have momentum." See: new momentum.

moms (the) = ignorant teenage serial producers of bastards at public expense; also their older sisters; See: single moms and teenage moms.

moral equivalency = *libtalk* for softening previously embraced evil into acceptability by saying the good guys really did things that were as bad or almost as bad as the so-called bad guys. e.g., U.S. vis-à-vis the Soviet Union in the Cold War. See: everyone does it.

most vulnerable = *gooeytalk* label used to describe those allegedly affected by any attempt to cut government spending programs no matter how outrageous in an effort to discredit it.

moving forward = *slickism* (unless supported by verifiable fact) to put a positive veneer on a dead-in-the-water situation; usually hedged with legalistic *slimeisms* such as "I think it would be fair to say" or "Many feel we are." See: making progress, encouraged.

move on (time to) = *willietalk* for urging a change of subject. See: healing process.

multiple fragment lacerations = *technogook* for shrapnel wounds, possibly fatal.

mystified = *willietalk* sugarcoating for denial of an accusation that has a high probability of being true.

See: bewildered.

N.

narrow definition = *willietalk* for the art of refining the description of something to the point where almost everything behind the label is removed but the label remains in place. This technique is most effective when auditors do not know about that the "refining." e.g., see sexual relations.

nation building = what used to be called in the 19th Century The White Man's Burden taken on by what now is called tolerant societies. See: restoring democracy.

Native American = Compassionate Stone Age Asian aborigines who took over North and South America several thousand years ago as opposed to hateful Europeans who started taking over 500 years ago.

Nazi = an ultimate *badguy label* used by hardcore liberal Democrats to describe Republicans favoring such legislation as a reduction in growth of school lunch programs.

Neanderthal = Originally chauvinistic caveman behavior ascribed by feminists to males who treat women as chattels rather than equals; now, particularly in lower case, used by feminist activists to describe any but the most wimpish male: particularly white males.

near-elderly = *willietalk* for almost-old, a pleasant sounding demographic category of people over 60 but under 65.

needy (the) = *gooeytalk* descriptor for a group that sometimes expands politically to include almost everyone who doesn't own his and hers BMWs, but often a *gooeytalk* synonym for the equally vague "the poor" or "the hungry." (See: both)

neutered = unpleasant but still preferable to castrated, sterilized or fixed; possibly may give way to sexually adjusted.

new = *adspeak* for any product that has not been promoted lately.

new momentum = something announced as being added to a meeting when there are no concrete results; sometimes further gussied up as forward momentum (presumably as opposed to reverse momentum). See: momentum.

night pay = *governmentspeak* for extra pay to government employees originally for work at night but later extended to employees who work normal but flexible shifts during daytime hours. See: official time.

no controlling legal authority = *goretalk spin* for no one has been indicted to date for this obviously sleazy and probably illegal act. This is also known as the Vice President Gore defense ploy used to excuse campaign fund raising from the White House.

no specific recollection = *willietalk* for something unpalatable that one is unable under oath to recall no matter how hard one tries.

non-permissive environment = political dove *spinspeak* for a totally hostile government and people who will start shooting at you if you try to land troops in their territory. See: peacekeepers.

non-person = Communist Bolshevik *commiespeak* for anyone targeted for killing without trial; obviously non-persons such as aristocrats, intellectuals, bourgeoisie, military officers, troublesome leftist ideologues and inconvenient Bolshevik competitors have no rights because they are by definition non-persons.

non-results oriented competition = athletic games played without keeping score to avoid the alleged embarrassment of having winners and losers as on "the playing fields of Eaton" where the Battle of Waterloo was reputed to have been won. See: recenter.

normal = a hate word that destroys the self-esteem of the non-normal and, therefore, must be abolished.

non-consensual physical contact = date rape or, depending on the circumstances, a change of mind.

non-emergency workers = upgraded description of government workers who were originally called non-essential and objected to the terminology.

non-paper = *spin* label for proposed document that you are trying to slip by critics until it is approved. (First used by radical American feminists with assistance of the Clinton Administration for their controversial "Draft Program for Action" planned as the basic discussion document at the UN World Conference on Women held in Beijing in 1995. See: gender perspective.

not forthcoming = *spinspeak* for lying under oath. See" mislead, evasive, not telling the truth, limited modified hangout.

not telling the truth = rather transparent *gooeytalk* for lie (sometimes softened more to telling less than the truth); employed to avoid being accused of using language beyond civil discourse or even perjury..

not to my knowledge = legalism meaning: I didn't do it; but, if you can prove that I did, you can't get me for perjury because I don't remember.

nurturing = *gooeytalk* for (1) a mysterious alchemy performed more likely than not on natural losers by well-paid workers in the Poverty Industry or (2) what used to be called taking care of your kids. See: parenting.

O.

Ooooooh = *introcode* voiced with sad, worldly wise forbearance designed to dismiss the latest allegation of vileness, criminality or both as some of the same old stuff and then top with some totally unsubstantiated countercharge; perfected by First Lady Hillary Clinton.

official government matters = *plastertalk* for White House strategy huddles to fight allegations of perjury, obstruction of justice and sexual profligacy and various other crimes and personal improprieties.

official time = *governmentspeak* for most desirable time spent by government employees on what is loosely called "union business" including lobbying -- time compensated by taxpayers but since it generally is unmonitored it is often used for shopping, handling household chores and second jobs. See: night pay.

old news = *category shift* characterizing some criminal act, outrage or gross embarrassment as being not worthy of further consideration because it was reported yesterday. Such reports often are the result of deliberate leaks by the perpetrators to preempt announcements by investigators.

on track = cuddly phrase used to assure your auditors that this is the point where you expected to be while not mentioning that the tracks ahead have been bombed.

See: peace process.

open and free elections = a showtime activity involving a huge number of people casting ballots that confirm a previously determined conclusion; usually -- but not always -- conducted in the Third World with UN observers.

oppositionist = Stalinist *commiespeak* for anyone critical of Stanlist policies and targeted as an enemy to be jailed or shot. Same as wrecker.

orientation = social *willietalk* for non-heterosexual behavior.

otherabled = formerly, handicapped; still more formerly, crippled, blind, deaf dumb. See: impaired, challenged

outreach meeting = major political fund raising event of questionable and possibly illegal character; first utilization in 1996 by Vice President Albert Gore to describe a meeting he attended in a Buddhist monastery in Los Angeles where the monks, sworn to a life of poverty, made large donations of dubious origin to the Democratic Party.

outsiders = a condition that must be prevented at any cost or unfairness to normal and exceptional people.

overreaching = *category shift* besmirching the policeman for doing his duty and seeking to make the criminal a victim. See: goes too far, aggressive.

P.

paid for = *spin* for justification of increases in government spending on the grounds that taxes already collected or to be collected for some other government programs now allegedly canceled will be used for this new program rather than returned to the taxpayers.

pain = as in "I feel your pain"; *willietalk* , usually accompanied with moist eyes and a gently bitten lip, designed to show great sympathy and personal sadness often demonstrated for reasons other than human charity. See: the gooey-talk, caring.

paradigm = *technogook* often used by speakers who don't know what it means to cast a veneer of intellectuality on whatever snake oil they are selling. Much favored in corporate, government and pundit circles.

paradigm shift = *corporatespeak inflator* for dropping a disastrous strategy and firing a bunch of losers to be replaced by a new team and strategy that may save the CEO from early retirement; also useful in explaining unexpected economic collapses.

parenting = *gooeytalk* for the basic biological function performed by most mammals for thousands of years called bringing up offspring. See: nurturing.

partisan = a negative descriptor for a politician (usually a Republican) who does not agree with you. See: bipartisan and principle.

partition = something that the Clinton Administration insisted was not happening when it sought a division of Bosnia into two independent countries made up of deadly enemies operating under a powerless national entity.

partnering = *bizschoolspeak* for establishing a working relationship with a company that you can not take over at least for the present.

Partnership for Peace = Clinton plan reneging at the time on NATO membership for Poland, other newly-freed Eastern Bloc nations

peace = a highly desirable (for most) but increasingly dubious state of human relations that probably, at best, is a brief truce or armistice with sporadic, deadly interruptions; e.g., terrorist suicide bombings, local shootouts, forced population shifts.

peacekeepers = pure *willietalk* for combat troops usually serving under bumbling UN command and inadequate rules of engagement; also, when capitalized, the name of the MX multi-warhead ICBM; still earlier, the Colt .45.

peacemakers = apparently through being in the official photo, any political leader who attends a meeting that favors peace; e.g., attendees at the Clinton-called one-morning quickie "Summit of the

Peacemakers" in 1996 at Sharm el-Sheikh that resulted in an agreement to issue a statement denouncing Muslim terrorism against Israel.

peace policy = appeasement.

peace process = a thin *figleaf* for interminable negotiations probably going nowhere. See: process

penalize = guilt-loaded, negative adjective implying that some action taken against the "underdog" classes is uncaring and mean spirited. One of the favorite "p words." See: punitive.

(the) people or the American people = *gooeytalk* all-inclusive group name purportedly for all American citizens but, in reality, only those citizens and welfare-supported non-citizens who subscribe to the Nanny State and the elitists who like to tell everyone else what to do with themselves excepted because they are so good and so smart. All others are mean-spirited, rich (regardless of income level) Enemies of the People.

(the) people's business = *willietalk* for an undefined something that investigators are keeping you from doing by insisting on asking a lot of questions about what you really have been doing.

(the) people's house = patriotic subset of *gooeytalk* for the White House, terminology usually invoked by the principal occupant or his defenders to obscure misconduct. .

people of color = everyone in the world except Caucasians and sometimes even some of them. (See: Hispanic)

people's republic = *commiespeak* for wolf-in-sheep's-clothing form of absolute dictatorship long favored and propagated by International Communism in the 20th Century; usually a colonial satellite of the former Soviet Union.

perjury = the ancient crime of lying under oath which perjurers almost always righteously and steadfastly deny committing -- particularly graduate students of *willietalk.*

phased air campaign = *willietalk* for incremental bombing, a technique which proved generally ineffective in the Viet Nam War. See: air campaign.

Physical responsibility = popular corruption favored particularly by populist leaders for the words "fiscal responsibility."

placement = jail for juveniles.

politically correct (PC) = label used to attempt to prohibit and ban anything that the user finds objectionable totally regardless of the rights of others; much favored among tenured academics who came of age in the 1960's.

political solution = compromised deal with bad guys, e.g., Munich.

politics of hate (division, fear, defeat, personal destruction, demonization, gridlock) = *willietalk* for what anyone says in opposition.

politics of meaning = pop psycho-philosophical gobbledygook calling for feel-good ethics and lots of social transfer payments; much admired by the Clinton White House.

politics of personal destruction = reverse *spinspeak* denunciation of the people you are aggressively trashing because they charged you with criminal and immoral acts of which you clearly appear guilty.

premiums, contributions = taxes.

pretty routine = *willietalk* used to minimize the seriousness or weight of some outrageous act or proposal. e.g., a decision enabling a fat cat campaign contributor to perform potential treason would be called pretty routine. Usually preceded by some legal-out *codetalk.*

pregnancy termination = abortion.

principle = explanation usually advanced by the mainstream liberal media as the basis for a conservative caving in to a liberal position. See: bipartisan and partisan.

privacy = *spinspeak* stonewall built around garbage in an effort to prevent its discovery.

private conduct = See privacy.

process = endless meetings often obscuring futility of

accomplishment and expectation of none; used to imply that some kind of highly controlled, technical procedure is involved.

pro-choice = the "right" to abortion including widespread use as a handy form of casual birth control, natural selection and ready solution for change of mind.

pro-life = anti abortion in most cases, sometimes all cases including giving birth to monsters, matricides, very close blood relatives and retarded bastards sired by psychopathic rapists.

protect = increasingly used *figleaf* for theft of some of your money and/or property in return for not stealing all of it and/or terminating your existence.

protected group = voting block legally and socially empowered with unmerited advantage because of historical abuse to some of the group members' long dead ancestors; usually works to the disadvantage of Americans of European ancestry no matter how well qualified.

protected species = forms of fauna all-but humanized that are sometimes undesirably in danger of extinction and sometimes desirably so.

protective function privilege = *governmentspeak gobbledegook* invented by the Clinton Administration to try to prevent Secret Service agents protecting the President from testifying in criminal investigations of presidential activities. The Clinton Administration argument was that allowing Secret Service agents to testify would cause squeaky-clean but apparently suicidal Presidents to stay away from the agents and thereby invite assassination.

proximity peace talks = diplomatic negotiations by a third-party negotiator between deadly enemies placed in separate rooms in the same building because they can't be expected to get along with each other in the same room; a desperate negotiating approach of the Clinton Administration to be able to claim some kind of settlement in Bosnia.

psych background = Clinton White House press guide rule designed to hide attempts to brainwash the public through secret briefings by the President to editors on agreement that they will only use the material as their own. (Called by the WH press secretary: "deeper than deep background."

public interest = whatever you want to do; not in the public interest is what someone else wants to do and you don't.

punitive = guilt-loaded, negative adjective implying that some action taken against the "underdog" classes is uncaring and mean spirited. One of the favorite "p words." See: penalize.

put behind us and move on = translation: we (I) don't want to discuss this embarrassing matter or we (I) don't want to do this, so let's change the subject; often prefaced by the time has come. (See).

put politics aside = *willietalk* for: forget your principles, just work together and do it my way. See: bipartisan.

put this behind us = *willietalk* for we really, really, really want to bury this very embarrassing topic.

racism = an historic white prejudice that can never be expiated and considered by many blacks and white liberals (particularly those in safe neighborhoods) to be full justification for any black anti-social behavior no matter how outrageous, criminal and evil.

racist = a Caucasian who suggests that a non-Caucasian of any variety and circumstance is somewhat lacking in any way.

rage = an uncontrollable condition that, when felt by members of a recognized minority group, fully justifies and excuses looting, murder and other assorted violent and pathological acts the least of which would be the use of foul and insulting language.

(the) reality is = introductory *spin* ("trust me, friends, this is the real skivvy") on a half-truth statement, smarmy misrepresentation or total falsehood.

reeducation = reform through slave labor in Communist China and the former Soviet Union. See: corrective labor.

recenter = arbitrary improvement of lowered, unsatisfactory performance by upward adjustment of the "average" to the center. Benefits claimed for recentering is building the self-esteem of failing students and "improving" test results for the socially disadvantaged (See). Also, see: non-results oriented competition.

reclaim family life = special use of *gooeytalk* to invoke victim status for oneself and block further questions if possible.

reconfiguration = truly foggy *willietalk* first used to describe what would in effect be offensive redeployment of troops previously and disastrously operating as United Nations peacekeepers in Bosnia. Referred to by British military as "crossing the Mogadishu line" in reference to the disastrous switch of the UN in Somalia from peacekeeping to nation building.

recovered memory = *pyscho-tecnogook* adopted as *psychobabble* for highly self-serving and therefore highly questionable facts recalled years--often decades--after the alleged event. See: repressed memory syndrome (RMS)

reengineering = massive firing in connection with the reorganization of a failing company. See: syns. restructuring, downsizing.

reflects our values = vaporous *slickism* attached to proposals that the speaker wishes to appear to be supporting and subsequently will reject on grounds that the never clearly defined "values" were not reflected after all; use of the motherhood word "values" to sucker the working public into continuing to pay for a grab-bag of freeloading social welfare programs.

rehabilitation = punishment and commitment to state psychiatric prisons, a process much favored in the former Soviet Union for dealing with political opponents; also, *libtalk* for a far more often than not laughable but feel-good process leading to early release from prison of various criminal threats to society.

reinventing government = particularly low content *goretalk* for implying major restructuring and downsizing of government to make it more cost effective while actually retiring some aging secretaries, cutting back the Pentagon and replacing experienced civil service managers with low-cost part-time kids; includes lavish spending on celebratory slick brochures and much use of outsourcing from large contributors.

remember = *spinspeak* for a very difficult process in which few can be expected to succeed particularly under oath. Fans, sycophants and retainers often award many brownie points for trying hard. See: memory.

repressed memory syndrome (RMS) = borrowed *psychobabble* phrase used to explain amazing sudden recall of long ago events that would appear to have newly found potential monetary, political or criminal exculpatory value or some combination of these. (See: recovered memory).

reproductively impaired = impotent.

reproductive rights = code for the "right" to abortion or to use fertility drugs to give birth to large litters at taxpayer expense. See: fertility regulation and pregnancy termination. Also choice.

Republican woman = someone whose accomplishments don't count as do those of Democratic liberal women.

resettlement = forced exportation to worker death camps in Nazi Germany. See: disinfection.

resident = NKVD (Soviet Union Intelligence) spy living in the West prior to World War II; most recalled and executed during the Stalinist purges.

responsibility (take full) = a badge of "leadership" that you pin on yourself while making sure everyone understands that you are just doing it because of your innate nobility and you shouldn't be blamed. See: buck stops here; mistake.

restoring democracy = at best bringing about a not blatantly corrupt election with a minimum of killings. This activity is usually performed by peacekeepers assigned to nation building in countries where experience in practicing democracy is all but unknown.

restructuring = reorganization almost always involving massive firing in times of deep financial difficulties. Because of connotations the word has been generally displaced first by reengineering, then downsizing, then rightsizng. (See)

restrictive placement = maximum security for juvenile.

revisionist = a Communist Party *commiespeak* description of any Communist it has decided is an enemy who should be destroyed or jailed.

rhetoric = pejorative label used to dismiss any argument with which you disagree.

(the) right thing to do = *willietalk* blessing for an action no matter how flawed; See: time has come.

right kind = *slickism* modifier used to appear to the innocent that you favor something that you loath; e.g., right kind of balanced budget or right kind of welfare reform, pure *willietalk* signaling to the faithful that you truly oppose both; has the added benefit of sounding like right stuff, a highly positive and admirable attribute. (See: reflects our values)

right thing to do = *plastertalk* used to justify questionable or challengable acts.

right wing conspiracy (vast) = *diabolictalk* designed by the Clinton White House to deflect public attention from mounting political scandals and criminal investigations of the Clinton Administration.

rights = a growing portfolio of legal claims to be given free just about anything and be protected from and compensated handsomely for all mischance.

rightsizing = massive firing and reorganization usually performed at times of deep financial trouble and corporate disarray. Formerly: downsizing, reengineering, restructuring. (See: all.)

robust bombing = Pentagon *technogook* for total destruction of all military capability.

rules = as in play by: like family values, these have a fine, high sounding ring but often beneath the shiny surface include many reservations, exceptions and *slickisms* depending on the speaker.

rush to judgment = *Halloweentalk* used to undercut with arch disdain common sense conclusions that only the most biased would reject.

S.

safe areas = free fire zones where refugees have been told by the UN that they would be protected.

sanitary engineer = phony badge word for garbageman; one of hundreds of inflated job titles designed to upgrade honest (and sometimes not so honest) work into the ranks of professionalism.

seamless integration = *bizschoolspeak* for real world morning-after bloodletting following a corporate merger.

searcher = a late 20th Century communicant with crystal readers, astrologists and other beaded guardians of occult gateways; often involved in the magic of chemical potions.

self-affirming environments = segregated dormitories, eating clubs and so forth which are politically correct as long as they are not for whites.

self-esteem = a worthwhile view of oneself that must be maintained at any price including among other social costs the erosion of morality, dumbing down of public education and destruction of the judicial system.

sensitive 90's guy = absolute wimp who tears up a lot. See: sensitivity.

sensitivity = mental impairment that prevents those so afflicted from using words that communicate accurate meaning; anything goes and is understandable somehow.

separation of church and state = values neutral conditions (See: values neutral)

serious progress = *inflator* for progress required since that word has become a *willietalk* placebo. See: making progress.

sex addiction = *spinspeak* (hyper *plastertalk)* free pass for womanizing and philandering no matter how gross, immoral and socially destructive.

sex lies = *spinology* assertion that lies about sex are not lies but something that "everyone does" to protect others from public criticism or embarrassment about consensual sexual relations between adults. Invoked by the Clinton defenders to excuse lying about fellatio performed on numerous occasions by a 21-year old intern on the President of the United States in the Oval Office of the White House. See: everyone does it

sex workers = whores (female and male).

sexile = college student who can't go back to his coed dorm room because the sexile's roommate is engaging in sexual exploration.

sexism = highly offensive prejudicial feelings and acts by

men against women but not such feelings and acts by women against men on grounds that they are fully justified by at least 10,000 years of abuse. See: Neanderthal.

sexual affair (deniable) = sexual activity not including copulation and preferably one in which only one partner is "serviced."

sexual alternatives = non-judgmental term for such pastimes as sodomy, necrophilia, bestiality to name a few.

sexual orientation = whatever turns you on is okey-dokey; a whitewash flag used to describe what used to be called deviant behavior. See: sexual preference.

sexual preference = the "Good Housekeeping seal of approval" for sexual perversions that would have made Caligula blush.

sexual relations (deniable) = *willietalk* invented and greatly favored by President William Jefferson Clinton for sexual coupling that excludes fellatio. See: inappropriate behavior.

shocked = *willietalk* popularized in the film *Casablanca* in which the police chief expresses "shock" to learn that gambling is going on at Rick's nightclub where the chief, of course, often gambles.

single mother (mom) = conniving unwed peasant positioned as a victim of society and supported by taxpayers for life; term often transmuted to single mom to gain added sympathy.

slavery = a despicable put-down of superior freedom-loving black humanists by greedy and lecherous white colonialists living in Virginia.

slash = *worldend-talk* for reduction in growth.

so what = *introcode* perfected by the Clinton Administration and its Democratic political allies to say the public does not -- and should not -- care any longer about a wide variety of transgressions, outrages, and criminal acts perpetrated its political leaders because at best they are not important in the "big picture" or at worst they are merely accepted minor offenses. See: everyone (everybody) does it.

social justice = erosion of the American dream through providing free rides and redistribution of assets from those who work to those who don't. (See: economic justice)

social promotion = educational administrative *technogook* for the public school practice to pass failing students to bolster their self- esteem. See: self-esteem

social security = *governmentspeak* for a wondrous pension program for all citizens and deserving immigrants with the exception in all justice of up to 80 percent of the population defined as the rich. In reality, a legalized Ponzi scheme based on increasingly heavy taxation of the direct and indirect earned income of all Americans except for many government workers with better programs paid for by the tax base. See: Medicare.

Socialist solidarity = *commiespeak* for Soviet Union colonialism.

socially disadvantaged = illiterate sociopath.

socially impaired = no legal means of support; the permanent underclass that is not responsible for its activities (also: socially challenged)

sooner rather than later = *willietalk* phrase used as a verbal seat cushion hurled from a fleeing auto into the path of the oncoming police motorcycles.

sorry = classic *willietalk* for "I am sorry that I have to say I'm sorry but now that I've said it let's just forget the whole thing." See: move on (time to).

socially impaired citizen = mugger, burglar, drug pusher, killer, welfare chisler.

special education = costly dumping ground invented by the public school education bureaucracy for primarily welfare-supported children with behavioral problems such as threatening teachers, preferring to sleep in class to doing minimal work, doing drugs and carrying weapons.

special interests = a pejorative describing any group in opposition to your position; sometimes called selfish special interests. (See: activists and citizens groups).

spending caps = price controls for the private sector; in the public sector, a legal lid put on additional spending sometime in the future. See: spending cuts.

spending cuts = fees, canceled or increased; or cuts in future highly bloated spending plans. No connection with reduction in actual spending.

spies = Stalinist *commiespeak* for one of the lowest circles of the Communist "Enemies of the State" Hell; counterrevolutionists were Party members who opposed the latest policy of the moment; spies worked for foreign powers intent on destruction of the Party and the Soviet Union.

spokesperson = politically correct *libtalk* for a spokesman who is not male. Presumably the same tin-ear nomenclature would be applied to other callings such as garbageman if that word had not already been upgraded to waste handler or waste engineer as a means of protecting professional self esteem. See: waitperson.

squeegee = intimidating-looking street vandal who between muggings enlivens city life further by providing unsolicited windshield cleaning of cars stopped at traffic lights for which payment is demanded with threatening gestures.

spiritual journey = a self-serving procedure by which the perpetrator of one or more heinous acts is converted into a grieving victim nobly undergoing great suffering while the perpetrator's accusers are thoroughly demonized; original victims of the perpetrator's acts are explained away, minimized and forgotten – particularly if they are dead.

stand with = willingness to be available at no or minimal risk for photo opportunities with deadly foes when they reach agreements that bet their careers, lives and countries.

State Archive of the Russian Federation = Central Archive of the October Revolution, repository of such secret records of the Communist Party as documentation on the murder of the Imperial Family in a cellar at Ekaterinburg.

strategic investment = *willietalk* for major new government social spending almost certain to involve an increase in the deficit or tax increases. See: contributions.

strategic ambiguity = Clinton Administration *gobbledegook* for foreign policy that sounds tough but leaves open enough holes to retreat through followed by enemy tanks, howling mobs or both.

strike = military *spinspeak* employed by normally liberal doves for a light show war without casualties – particularly American casualties; such wars called by critics "TV infotainement" and "immaculate coercion."

substantive due process = interpretation of the "due process" clause of the US Constitution that it somehow contains some rights that ought to be there but just were not mentioned.

surgical strike = Pentagon *spinspeak* for bombing that through technology, skill and reasonable luck will hit only a military target while avoiding destruction of highly photogenic hospitals, orphan asylums and condominiums occupied by senior citizens.

sympathetic detonation = *technogook* for setting off larger explosions with human bombs. e,g., explosion of mines or bombs caused by explosion of human grenades; Japanese kamikazes diving into U.S. carriers in World War II.

T.

take down = Pentagon spinspeak for blow up while implying nothing more harmful than orderly disassembly, e.g., "We took down two refineries, one power plant and six barracks."

tax incentive = federal subsidy more than likely made more trouble than its worth when you read the fine print.

taxes = money belonging to the government which it earned by arbitrarily taking it from its citizens and knows best how to spend in their behalf.

team player = originally *corporatespeak* with some substance among true believers and players in team sports but now mostly *vacuumtalk* in all endeavors for don't make trouble and do what you're told.

teenage moms = unwed welfare-collecting mass producers of children by men of undetermined whereabouts, See: the moms, single mothers

temporary = an indeterminate period of time that sounds reasonably brief and terminable, but increasingly becoming a *figleaf* for semi-permanent to forever.

terrorist = crazy right-wing religious murderer unless he (she?) is a freedom fighter on your side.

the hungry = *gooeytalk* descriptor for an ill-defined group of the needy (See:)

the middle class = all hard-working Americans except the rich (whom the middle class join for tax purposes) and the very poor.

the needy = ill-defined lower stratum of society but by definition all beneficiaries of welfare. (See: the poor)

the neighborhoods = where tax money is spent to help the working people and the poor.

the poor = a growing, upwardly shifting and increasingly shiftless population supported by primarily by taxes transferred by the government from the rich; by definition, the poor can never become the middle class no matter how much money they receive because all monetary aid transferred is not counted as income.

the Poverty Industry complex = huge conglomeration of public and private sector people whose livelihood is directly tied to having a permanent, growing dependent population of the poor.

the rich = *badguy label* for selfish, greedy people who in reality are in the tax base that includes everyone except the poor. Self-excluded from this definition are compassionate Hollywood and TV stars and executives, millionaire elitist liberals, fat-cat political contributors and tenured, high-paid liberal academics. See: very wealthy third way = *phony badge* label for taking a fuzzy but very comforting political position just left of center between socialism and nanny big government on one side and capitalistic free markets and personal responsibility on the other.

thug = underground fighter for opposing side in struggle between autocratic regimes. See: freedom fighter.

time has come = codeword justification for almost any nut-cake policy; popular *wiilietalk* used in a variety of statements all starting: "The time has come to..."

time to move on = *bravebabble* for change the subject because this one is a real loser; also carries implication that somehow whatever outrage is under discussion is really quite trivial in the great scheme of things and has already been properly dealt with verbally but, of course, non-consequentially.

to the best of my knowledge = *codetalk* introducing a *willietalk* explanation of unfortunate events. Syns: as I recall, my recollection is. Preceding bunkum such as "It happened a long time ago but...." Often is used to play for sympathy particularly among those who truly have impaired memories.

tobacconist statue = cigar store Indian.

tolerant society = one of the "kinder, gentler" industrialized and mostly democratic powers who try to run the lives of their citizens with the citizens' money. (See: nation building.)

tough decisions = attribute assigned to whatever you want to justify regardless of character

thoughtful = *willietalk* adjective for delay as in: "We share your goal (e.g., balancing the federal budget) but instead of your program to accomplish it we need a thoughtful program yet to be developed. Often used in combination with very or even very, very to indicate that the culmination of the thinking process will take may take many years if indeed such a culmination is possible which, by implication, is in doubt.

transfer payments = legalized theft.

traumatic amputation = violent loss of a body part, e.g., left foot blown off.

tribute package = *corporatespeak* for a mawkishly nostalgic "high school-type" class year book passed out to employees by a corporation that has willing been acquired to the great financial benefit of top management and is in the process of severing thousands of its employees.

trophy brigade = one of many officially and unofficially. blessed groups of Soviet Union looters of art and other valuables that followed the Red Army into Germany in 1945 in the final days of World War II. The Soviets put the art "in temporary keeping" to "protect it" (See: temporary, protect), a condition that in many cases has continued through the remainder of the 20th Century.

troubled initiative = unethical or possibly illegal act.

U.

uncanny accident = military *plastertalk* for rocket bombing a civilian target. e.g., hitting a bridge as a civilian train is crossing it.

unearned income = what some economists still regard as money earned by capital investment is more generally defined pejoratively as illegitimate gleanings that support polo players even when they are 89-year old widows. (See: earned income)

unindicted coconspirator = a previously very reluctant prosecution witness who lives in hope that the prosecutor will find him worthy of not being moved to the defendant's table.

unfortunate colonial experience = revisionist liberal historian terminology for the spread of Western Civilization -- particularly to the former African colonies now enjoying the blessings of military dictatorships that have brought them ruthless exploitation, starvation and genocide.

universal = *willietalk* rubber-word originally meaning "all Americans" but subsequently to mean 95 percent; 90 percent or less; or plans to affect most Americans on some distant future date.

universal health care = socialized medicine

untimely pregnancy = *plastertalk* for carrying an illegitimate child.

UNPFOR = poorly led regular troops from various countries operating under the flag and direction of the UN civilian bureaucracy.

unwelcome overture = *spinspeak* for such private conduct as the executive dropping of one's trousers before a subordinate woman employee and suggesting fellatio. See privacy and sexual relations (deniable).

V.

values = often deliberate obfuscation of value neutral thinking, e.g. the *willietalk* proposition "we must protect our values" without identifying what they are.

value migration = *bizschoolspeak* for changing corporate culture from say gooey-feely in a boom economy to something like crush-the-bastards in a time of economic distress.

value neutral = *libtalk* for totally amoral usually accompanied with an aggressive abhorrence of any condemnation of anti-social conduct.

values clarification = the "clarification" under this teaching philosophy is that right and wrong are both okey-dokey depending on your viewpoint. (See: value neutral)

vast right-wing conspiracy = *diabolictalk* made famous by First Lady Hillary Clinton in seeking to counter the alleged spreaders of scandalous stories about President Clinton.

verbal conduct = *libtalk* mind police phrase for the hate crime of saying anything not considered to be politically correct by the elitist auditors while insisting on First Amendment protection solely for the leftist elect and its client Victim Community.

See: hate

verifier = *inflator* for international observer with questionable back up assigned augustly to some trouble spot by some international group to prove to world opinion that everything is okey-dokey now all despite appearances.

very wealthy = a pejorative for just what it says, but, in fact, an inclusive word sweeping in everyone including two income families who once were considered members of the middle class. Not included: compassionate Hollywood millionaires and other wealthy but penitent liberals. See: the rich.

vital center = an undefined marshland where little occurs and mediocre and indecisive leadership is always honored. (See: common ground)

victim = a descriptor for a continuing state of blamelessness for whatever you do no matter how malignant; often includes demonization of those you harm; or someone who lacks something (e.g., money, good luck, beauty, intelligence) through the vagaries of society and/or genetics. See: deprived.

victory = cotton-candy political claim of often only the most minor validity -- particularly when used in connection with foreign affairs..

Viet Nam War = one of the major conflicts in the 50-year Cold War that is an increasingly difficult subject for aging non-combatant American political opponents to discuss. (See: Cold War.)

vigilante = any armed citizen who defends himself successfully against muggers, rapists, looters, killers, arsonists and robbers.

vulnerable = *gooeytalk* for anyone receiving welfare. See: most vulnerable.

W.

waitperson = politically correct *libtalk* used by socially neutered waiters and waitresses to describe their occupations as in the sentence "I am Wanda (Steve), your waitperson." See: spokesperson.

war criminal = increasingly a *cry-wolftalk* label used against ruthless enemy heads of state and their associates particularly when they run less powerful countries or are not related to a protected U.S. minority.

war crimes = increasingly *diabolictalk* phrase being emptied of original meaning through over use by politicians and their followers who lack understanding that, unlike TV movies, wars involve lots of real people becoming really dead. See: genocide, war criminal.

warrior = Neanderthal professional killer unless you are talking about warriors like the peace-loving Native Americans who defeated Custer. See: military.

War in the Pacific (the) = Mid-20th Century conflict waged savagely by the United States against a nation usually unnamed in order not to offend anyone. See: event.

WASP = particularly vicious and dangerous category of whites who have been eating with knives, forks and table linen for at least two generations. (See:)

way beyond = *inflator* for more extreme than excessive.

we = *fogword* used to imply that some vague group – not just the speaker alone – committed whatever offense is under discussion; in fact, the speaker only learned about it afterward, probably only when asked about it.

Welfare Industry = Vast and growing conglomeration of professionals, semi-professionals and quasi-professionals along with the usual army of bureaucratic hangers-on and layabouts whose livelihood depends for justification on maintaining a large population on the public dole. See: Poverty Industry.

white male = red neck chauvinist pig church burner. See: angry white males.

whites = self-serving, mean-spirited descendants of evil European exploiters of kindhearted people of color throughout the world. See: WASP.

wiggle room = *cutespeak* for speaking with forked tongue.

woman = a victimized minority person usually with a low opinion of men. (See: Republican woman.)

work together = A Trojan Horse phrase calling for action and clearly implying that if you don't agree with me you aren't willing to work together.

work of the people (the people's work) = vaguely defined activity which the Clintonistas say the "the people" elected the President to do. See: the people.

working families = everyone except the rich and the poor.

(the) workers' paradise = favorite Communist Party *commiespeak* sobriquet for the now-collapsed Soviet Union and the worldwide heavenly promise of International Communism expected momentarily along with worldwide revolution of the workers.

working people = what used to be meant in the United States by blue collar class but the cut-off point slides upwards or downwards depending on audience and intent; also See: middle class.

wrong-doing = blurry *spinspeak* for criminal activity; attempt to confuse such actions as fraud, theft, suborning judges with being unkind to animals and failing to clean up your room.

Y.

Y2K = *corporatespeak technogook* for a computer software problem that, although mostly solved, must be understood to continue to have the potential of dooming mankind in order to maintain full lucrative employment of the Y2K Problem Correction Industry. As the problem continues to fade, it is sure to be adopted as *goretalk* and a form of *Halloweentalk.*

ABOUT THE AUTHOR

James Baar is a writer, international communications consultant, journalist, corporate communications software developer, a business executive and college lecturer. He is the author of a satirical novel on business and public affairs, *The Great Free Enterprise Gambit*, and four books on politics and technology. He lives in Providence, RI.

www.ingramcontent.com/pod-product-compliance
Lightning Source LLC
Chambersburg PA
CBHW020538290526
45786CB00002B/946